OCS Study
MMS 2002-038

Outer Continental Shelf Pipelines Crossing the Louisiana Coastal Zone: A Geographical Information System Approach

Final Report

I0439103

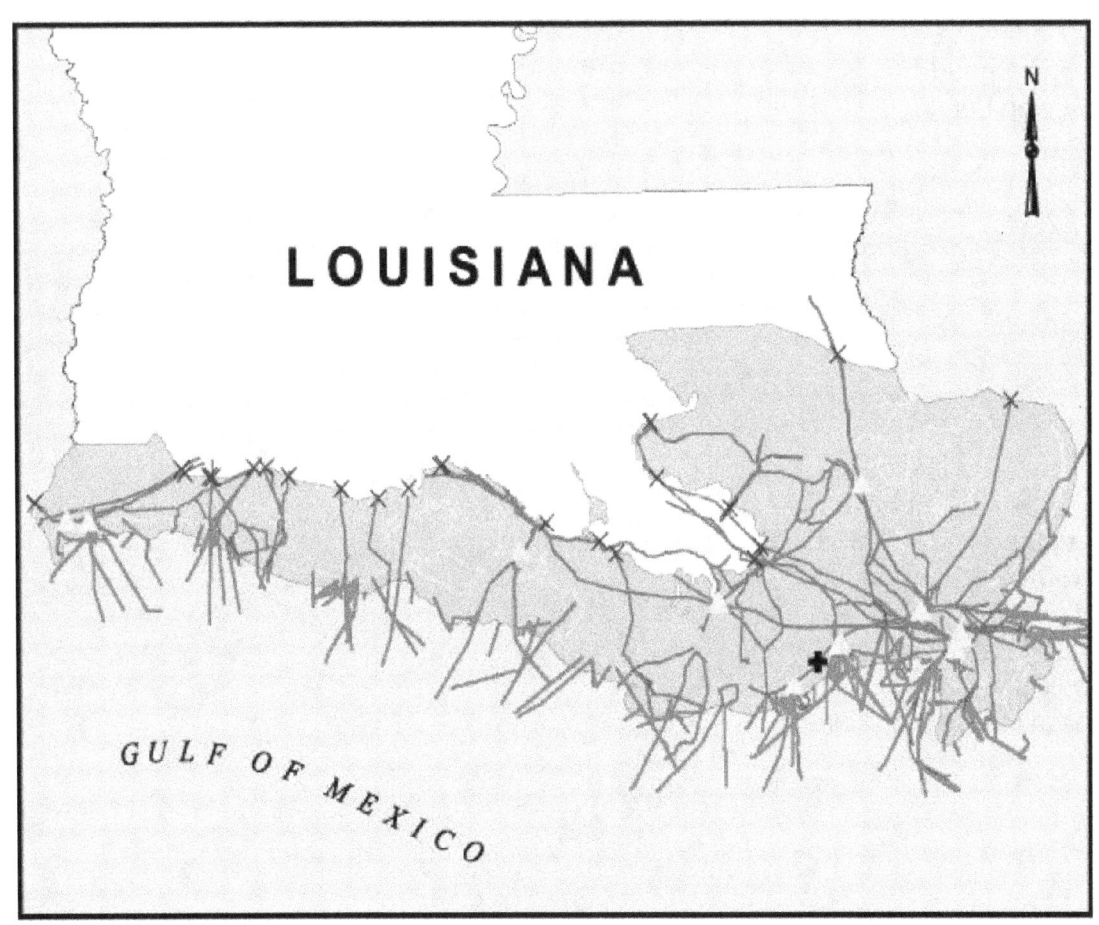

MMS

U.S. Department of the Interior
Minerals Management Service
Gulf of Mexico OCS Region

OCS Study
MMS 2002-038

Outer Continental Shelf Pipelines Crossing the Louisiana Coastal Zone: A Geographic Information System Approach

Final Report

Authors

R. Hampton Peele
John I. Snead
Weiwen Feng

Prepared under MMS Cooperative Agreement
1435-01-98-CA-30895
by
Louisiana Geological Survey
Louisiana State University
Baton Rouge, Louisiana

Published by

U.S. Department of the Interior
Minerals Management Service
Gulf of Mexico OCS Region

New Orleans
August 2002

DISCLAIMER

This report was prepared under a cooperative agreement between the Minerals Management Service (MMS) and Louisiana State University. This report has been technically reviewed by the MMS, and it has been approved for publication. Approval does not signify that the contents necessarily reflect the views and policies of the MMS, nor does mention of trade names or commercial products constitute endorsement or recommendations for use. It is, however, exempt from review and compliance with the MMS editorial standards.

REPORT AVAILABILITY

Extra copies of this report may be obtained from the Public Information Office (Mail Stop 5034) at the following address:

U.S. Department of the Interior
Minerals Management Service
Gulf of Mexico OCS Region
Public Information Office (MS 5034)
1201 Elmwood Park Boulevard
New Orleans, Louisiana 70123-2394

Telephone: (504) 736-2519 or
                        1(800) 200-GULF

CITATION

Suggested citation:

Peele R.H., J.I. Snead, and W. Feng, 2001. Outer Continental Shelf Pipelines Crossing the Louisiana Coastal Zone: A Geographic Information System Approach. Final Report. OCS Study MMS 2002-038. Prepared by the Louisiana Geological Survey, Louisiana State University. U.S. Dept. of the Interior, Minerals Management Service, Gulf of Mexico OCS Region, New Orleans, LA. 40 pp.

ABOUT THE COVER

The cover illustration depicts the specific pipeline network of the Louisiana Coastal Zone and the adjacent MMS Outer Continental Shelf Area, which was compiled in GIS format at LGS, during this study.

Preface

This Final Report summarizes the procedures, results, conclusions, and recommendations reached as a result of the preparation of the deliverables for the project, "Research, Compilation, and Digitization of Problematical and Uncontrolled Source Maps for the Louisiana Statewide Oil and Gas Pipeline Digital Database". Some of the tasks and approaches evolved during the course of the project and are documented below. All pipelines possessed in digital format by the Louisiana Geological Survey (LGS) and the Minerals Management Service (MMS), including those pipelines added as a result of this project, were reviewed in the process of developing the deliverable geographic information system (GIS) data products. However, it should be noted that there might be other pipelines in the study area as yet undocumented and therefore not usable in this project. The final deliverable GIS data products only include the MMS Outer Continental Shelf (OCS) pipelines that cross the Louisiana boundary into the Louisiana Coastal Zone (LCZ), the available LGS Outer Continental Shelf (OCS) related pipelines, and the LCZ termini associated with these pipelines.

Acknowledgments

This project could not have been made without the contributions of a number of people from Louisiana State University. We thank our Graduate Assistants Steven Rainey, Ahmet Binselam, Mohuidin Shaik, Andrew Beall and Louis Temento for their work in the completion of many of the primary tasks of the project.

We appreciate the assistance of Robert Paulsell, who shared data and source material from his concurrent project to gather information about undocumented and abandoned pipelines in south Louisiana. Thanks also go to Fred Kring and Syed Haque for Global Positioning System (GPS) field truthing of coastal zone pipelines.

Much indirect support of the project through graphics preparation, telephone contacts, data sharing, equipment maintenance, and other lab and office help was provided by LGS cartographic staff Bud Millet, Lisa Pond, David Griffin; and student worker Shannon Rabalais.

Thanks also go to the administrative staff of the Louisiana Geological Survey. Director Chacko John, contracts and grants reviewer Tommy Hill, accountant Carla Domingue, and office coordinator Ann Tircuit were of direct help on the project.

The authors especially wish to thank our MMS COTRs, Samuel Holder and Mary Boatman. They have been extremely professional and helpful to us in the performance of their duties, as Contract Technical Representatives, for this MMS contract.

R. Hampton Peele
John I. Snead
Weiwen Feng

Summary

The Minerals Management Service (MMS) is required to acquire information on the existing onshore oil and gas infrastructure, which services the Outer Continental Shelf (OCS) offshore industry. Pipelines are a major part of this infrastructure and constitute the principal transportation system for natural gas, crude oil, refined petroleum products, and certain liquid commodities such as sulfur and brine.

Geographic Information System (GIS) technology provides MMS with a powerful tool for analysis of transportation, environmental impact, and emergency response issues. However, such analysis awaits completion of an accurate, large-scale digital pipeline model as the basis for much important derivative research. In addition MMS has a need to document the routes of OCS-related pipelines ashore to either (1) the northern Louisiana Coastal Zone (LCZ) boundary, (2) neighboring states, (3) tanker terminals, or (4) refineries, and to characterize those termini.

This project has allowed the MMS to make use of the Louisiana pipeline GIS data currently being developed by the Louisiana Geological Survey (LGS). When the project began, these data were geospatial linear features with graphic text labels. LGS also had 118 source maps from pipeline operators that contained inadequate geospatial control information. Geospatial control was first established on the 118 uncontrolled, operator-supplied, source maps in the early period of the project. Geospatial control was also established on an additional 96, newly acquired pipeline maps. Then, they were digitized and compiled. A total of 214 source maps submitted to LGS from 15 pipeline companies were investigated in this project.

Task 1 of the project was to evaluate these inadequate source maps and to research the best techniques for establishing geospatial control.

Task 2 established geospatial control on all of the 118 in-house source maps. Seven different techniques were employed, as needed, depending on the characteristics of the source map.

Task 3 involved the digitization of the 118 in-house source maps plus 96 new maps, the compilation of a digital mosaic, and merger of the digital mosaic with the digital LGS pipeline data.

Task 4 was to investigate the LGS pipelines and the MMS pipelines around the LCZ boundary. All LGS pipelines crossing the LCZ and interconnecting with MMS pipelines were identified and edge-matched with the MMS pipelines. The database for the pipeline linear features was populated with information from the operator's source maps using the MMS prescribed database definition. The pipeline linear features were then segmented. ArcView GIS 3.1/3.2 was used for all of Task 4.

Task 5 was an investigation of the pipeline termini within the LCZ boundary. All pipelines transporting materials between the OCS and the LCZ were traced by studying the operator's source maps and the results from the GPS field surveying. During field investigations, Global Position System (GPS) positions of the pipeline termini were collected using a Magellan Mark Pro X DGPS receiver. The pipeline attribute data were collected through field investigations, trade directories, and telephone contacts. These OCS pipeline termini in the LCZ include tanker terminals, refineries, points where pipelines enter neighboring states, and points where pipelines cross the northern coastal-zone boundary. Attribute data of the pipeline termini includes termini identification codes, operator's names, locations, parishes, mailing addresses, contact phone numbers, and fax numbers depending on availability. The GPS data were downloaded into a computer workstation, converted into ArcView GIS shapefiles; then, the attribute data tables were populated. The LGS pipeline exit points on both Louisiana/Texas and Louisiana/Mississippi boundaries and the LCZ northern border were also identified, geocoded, and included in the pipeline termini ArcView shapefile. Data on tanker terminals and refineries are compiled and reported. Only those pipelines originating in the OCS areas and entering the LCZ, which have been reported to either the LGS and or the MMS, by pipeline operators, were traced and reported in this study.

Table of Contents

List of Figures

List of Tables

1.0 Executive Summary

Background

The existing crude oil, natural gas, and refined product pipeline maps of Louisiana are outdated, limited by small scale, and contain a number of significant errors. The Louisiana Geological Survey (LGS) has an ongoing program to gather accurate, large-scale maps and engineering diagrams directly from the pipeline operators to create a reliable, large-scale digital pipeline map and spatial database for statewide GIS applications. A large number of these source maps were uncontrolled, schematic, small-scale, and otherwise problematic. These maps were unsuitable for GIS database entry without extensive source research, geo-referencing, and/or field investigation, which was considered outside the scope of the original project.

In this project, LGS compiled these problematical pipeline maps and prepared them for inclusion in the statewide pipeline GIS as well as for further consideration within this study. In addition, the LGS tracked the OCS-originating pipelines into the onshore pipeline network and investigated their termini, within the Louisiana Coastal Zone (LCZ).

The Louisiana Geological Survey has been designated to serve as the Louisiana State Repository for the National Pipeline Mapping System (NPMS). The NPMS is a multi-agency Federal program initiated and sponsored by the U.S. Department of Transportation, Office of Pipeline Safety in 1999. It is an effort to establish a national pipeline GIS and mapping system. New and updated pipeline data and source maps covering the entire Louisiana Coastal Zone will be received from most of the Louisiana pipeline operators, during this five-year project, ending in 2003. However, new NPMS data did not arrive in time for inclusion in this project.

Rationale

It is fundamental to obtain accurate and up-to-date digital pipeline maps for governmental planning and decision-making applications in natural resource management, emergency preparedness management and environmental risk assessment. High-quality pipeline mapping also provides vital basic data needed to enable subsequent derivative research regarding pipeline environmental impacts and transportation planning issues. This vital information on the existing onshore infrastructure that serves the offshore petroleum industry will provide MMS with high-quality data for use in GIS analysis for risk management, environmental impacts, and engineering planning.

The LGS effort to complete onshore coverage of the pipeline GIS is in concert with the current MMS effort to tie their existing OCS pipeline GIS data to pipelines in state waters. The project enables MMS to follow the OCS-originating pipelines to the onshore pipeline network in the LCZ where documented digital pipeline data exists.

Methods

The project has five major phases:

1   Evaluating existing inadequate source maps and research to determine best method of problem resolution. Some archival research and field investigation of poorly documented pipelines was necessary.

2   Establishing spatial control (geo-referencing) for the existing uncontrolled source maps. The problems addressed include detail level, map projections, edge-matching, and cartographic error.

3   Digitizing and GIS compilation of the pipeline map data.

4   Edgematching, segmenting and merging the LGS pipeline data to the MMS/OCS pipeline data set.

5   Identifying onshore, OCS-related pipeline termini.

Results

A seamless coverage of OCS pipelines across the state/federal boundary is the resulting product. Geodetic control was established for 118 uncontrolled, operator-supplied source maps. A total of 214 in-house source maps from 15 companies were digitized and compiled into the LGS digital pipeline system. The LGS pipeline data were merged with the MMS/OCS pipeline data to meet the MMS database definition and format specifications. All edgematching adjustments were made under MMS advisement.

The LGS pipeline attribute data, derived from 124 source maps submitted by pipeline operators, were entered into the database in ArcView GIS 3.1/3.2. All OCS-related pipelines were traced from their origins in the OCS to terminus. Locations of the pipeline termini were determined, collected and verified by GPS field surveying, and transformed into an ArcView GIS shapefile. The findings of this project are listed below:

- 191 of the OCS pipelines pass through the state/federal (Louisiana) boundary. 150 of these pipelines pass through the Federal/Louisiana boundary and apparently do not connect with LGS pipelines. It remains uncertain if they connect with any onshore pipelines due to incomplete pipeline data for Louisiana. Therefore, their termini are considered unknown. 41 of the 191 have been digitally connected to onshore, LGS pipelines. This accounts for 21% of the total number of OCS pipelines reaching the Federal/State boundary.

- 1 OCS/LGS pipeline crosses the Louisiana Coastal Zone and exits at the Texas/Louisiana boundary.

- 1 OCS/LGS pipeline crosses the Louisiana Coastal Zone; and exits at the Mississippi/Louisiana boundary.

- 21 OCS/LGS pipelines cross the Louisiana Coastal Zone; and exit at the Louisiana Coastal Zone northern boundary.

- 19 OCS/LGS pipelines enter the Louisiana Coastal Zone and terminate at facilities therein.

    Facility types: 1. Refineries   4

                                  2. Tanker Terminals   15

- 7 OCS/LGS onshore pipelines pass through the Federal/Louisiana boundary, and cannot be paired with any OCS pipelines. They appear to be missing from the MMS pipeline GIS database.

2.0 Introduction

2.1 Description

This is a study of the transmission pipelines in the Louisiana Coastal Zone (LCZ) that originate in the Outer Continental Shelf (OCS) area of the Gulf of Mexico. The Louisiana Geological Survey (LGS) has developed a substantial, though incomplete, digital mapping system of onshore Louisiana pipelines. In this study, these LGS data were adapted to the format maintained by the Mineral Management Service (MMS), and spatially corrected to result in compatible geographic information system (GIS) data for the OCS-related pipelines in the LCZ. The related onshore pipeline termini that occur in the LCZ were characterized as part of the study. As a result of this collaborative project, the pipeline databases in both MMS and LGS organizations have been enhanced. With the proper utilization of these GIS databases, they could prove to be valuable in the areas of governmental regulatory (permitting) activities as well as emergency planning and response coordination. The substances transported by the pipelines are categorized into three types: natural gas, crude oil, and refined products. The nominal diameters of the pipelines were rounded to nearest integers.

2.2 Study Area

The study area of this project includes the LCZ and OCS areas off the coast of Louisiana (Figure 1.1). Due to the odd shape of the Louisiana Coastal Zone, several OCS pipelines leave the area and later re-enter. Those pipelines that exit and later re-enter the LCZ are included in the product.

2.3 Terminology

A *transmission pipeline* is defined as a pipeline that transports crude oil, natural gas, or product in bulk. Neither gathering system pipelines, nor distribution pipelines are considered transmission pipelines, for the purpose of this study.

An *OCS pipeline* is defined as a pipeline originating in the Outer Continental Shelf (OCS) area of the Gulf of Mexico.

An *OCS-related pipeline* refers to a pipeline in the LCZ that is linked with OCS pipelines.

An *operator source map* is defined as the hardcopy plats, "as-builts," engineering diagrams, and system maps, that have been provided to either LGS or MMS, by the pipeline operators.

A pipeline *terminus* is defined as an oil and gas processing facility, storage facility, or intermodal transport facility in the Louisiana Coastal Zone where an OCS-related pipeline ends delivery of petroleum oil and gas, or connects with an onshore transmission pipeline. In this study, the exit points of pipelines leaving the LCZ were identified and reported as a special type of termini, "Exit," in the GIS database.

A pipeline *endpoint* represents the point at which the pipeline tracing ends. These points fall into two categories, pipeline "interconnections" and pipeline "termini."

An *interconnection* refers to the point where an OCS-related pipeline intersects an onshore transmission pipeline. Measurement and regulation stations are often tie-in facilities conducting volume measurement or similar functions where a pipeline system transfers products to another pipeline system.

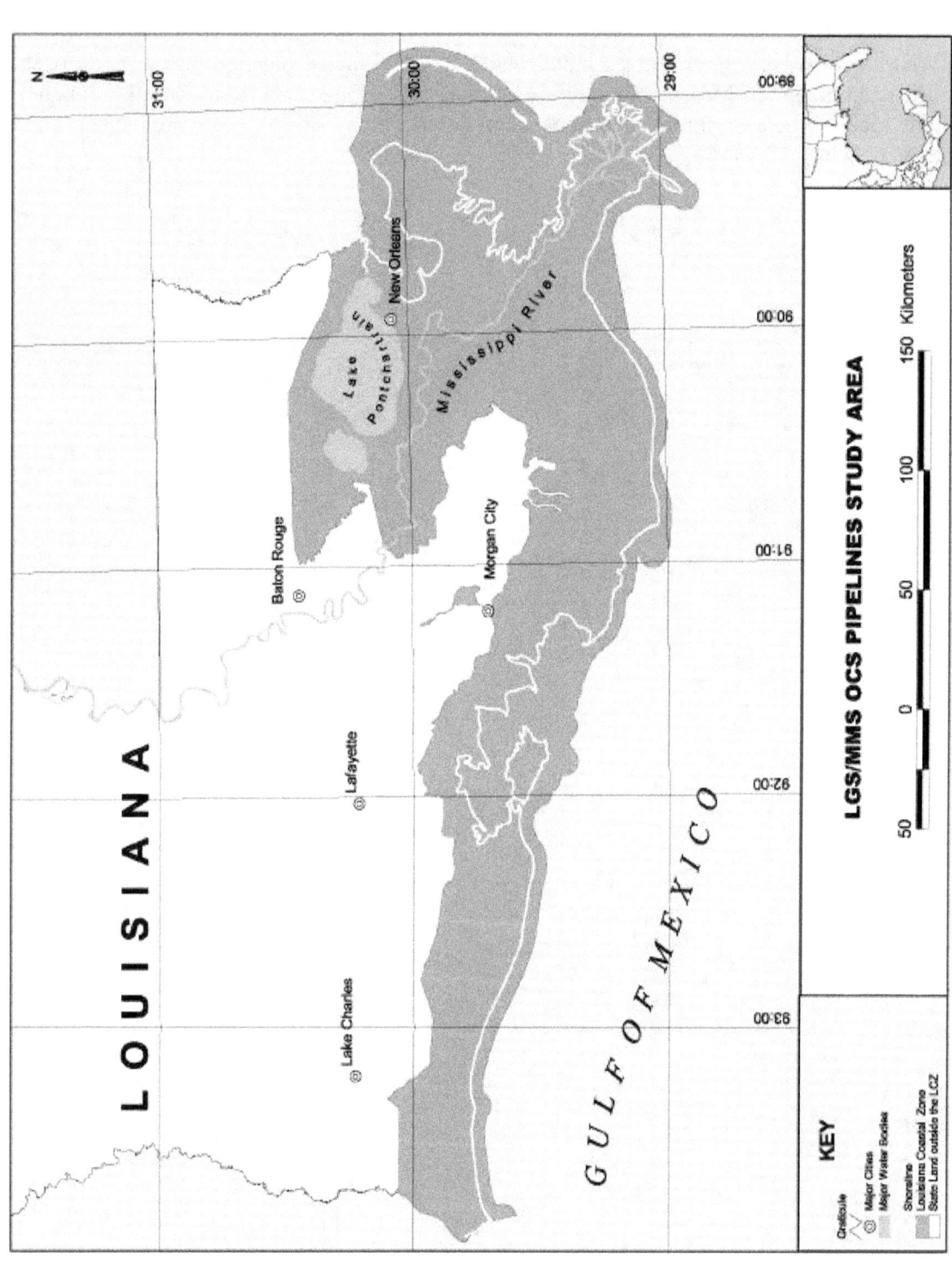

Figure 1.1 Project Study Area

3.0 Methodology

3.1 Task 1 - Evaluation of Existing Inadequate Source Maps

The earliest work on the project was the evaluation of the existing problematic source maps and the research to determine best methods of problem resolution. This involved contacting the pipeline operators who had submitted inadequate reference maps to LGS in order to obtain better data, if possible, from the original source. It also involved research of government records, environmental permits, aerial and satellite imagery, third-party maps and documents, as well as library and Internet references. The problem was complicated by the existence of numerous abandoned pipelines that are usually out of date, out of service, lack documentation and have missing records. Field GPS investigations of problematic facilities were conducted and ground-truthing data were collected.

A few maps submitted were of very small scale (less than 1:3,000,000) and diagrammatic in nature and were completely unusable. However many were maps of adequate scale and accuracy, just lacking good geodetic control points for digitization. This effort identified 118 problematic maps that were considered usable if proper geospatial control could be established.

3.2 Task 2 - Establishing Spatial Control for Existing Uncontrolled Source Maps

Geo-spatial control was established on each of the 118 initially uncontrolled source maps. Seven different techniques were used, as needed, depending on the characteristics of the source map. The most accurate technique available was employed for each source map. The order of preference for technique selection was as follows:

1. Unlabelled graticule cross-tics shown on the source map were identified by finding corresponding cross-tics shown on one or more USGS 1:24,000 scale minute quadrangle maps. This was done by visual comparison of landforms depicted on both maps. The coordinates of the USGS cross-tics were then assigned to the cross tics on the source maps.

2. Unlabelled graticule cross-tics shown on the source map were identified by finding corresponding cross-tics shown on Louisiana DOTD Parish Highway Maps (less than 1:24,000 scale). This was done by visual comparison of landforms depicted on both maps. The coordinates of the DOTD cross-tics were then assigned to the cross-tics on the source maps.

3. The geo-coordinates for the starting point (0+00) of a surveyed pipeline, as drawn on a surveyor's "as-built" diagram, was determined by first identifying that same point on another previously digitized source map. That point could then be located in the digital version of the previously digitized source map, so that the coordinates of that point could be reported by the GIS software. These coordinates were then used to place the starting point of the surveyed pipeline from the surveyor's "as-built" diagram. From this coordinate, the remainder of the pipeline was digitized by keyboard input of the bearings and distances reported on the "as-built" diagram.

4. Geo-coordinates for Public Land Survey System (PLSS) section corners on the source map were determined by finding corresponding intersections on one or more USGS 7.5

minute Digital Line Graphs (DLGs). This was done by visual comparison of the PLSS lines depicted on both maps. If a section corner was not available in the partially complete USGS 7.5 minute DLG series, the section corner was digitized from the appropriate USGS 7.5 minute quadrangle map. Then the coordinates of the selected intersections were assigned to the corresponding corners on the source map.

5. Intersections of linear features and landforms, having acute angles in their shapes, were selected as possible control points on the source maps, if they could be located accurately on USGS 7.5 minute quadrangle maps. These intersections and shapes were digitized from the USGS Quads. The coordinates of the intersection and the vertices of the acute angles in the shapes were reported by the GIS software. These coordinates were then assigned to the corresponding points on the source maps for use as control.

6. Euclidean geometric techniques of extending lines to create intersections in the margins, bisecting lines, triangulation, etc., were used in precisely the same way on both the source map and on the corresponding USGS 7.5 minute quadrangle map to create control points. The techniques employed were not scale specific. The points created on the USGS quad map were digitized; and their coordinates were reported in the GIS software. These coordinates were then assigned to the corresponding points that had been created on the source map.

7. Intersections of linear features were selected as possible control points on the source maps. GPS positions were collected in the field at the ground locations of these possible control points. These coordinates were then applied to the corresponding points on the source maps.

3.3 Task 3 - Digitization and Compilation of the Pipeline Map Data

The 118 pipeline operator source maps were digitized using the control points established in Task 2. An additional 96 pipeline source maps, recently acquired by LGS from operators, were found to be in the coastal zone. These source maps had adequate control points and were digitized as well. All 214 digitized pipeline operator source maps were then compiled into company mosaic files, and edgematched. Digital Matrix InfoCAD GIS software was used to perform the digitizing, mosaic compilation and edgematching.

3.4 Task 4 - Integration of LGS and MMS Pipeline Data Sets

The LGS pipeline data were merged with the MMS/OCS pipeline data to meet the MMS database definition and format specifications. All LGS pipeline linear features that do not enter the Outer Continental Shelf were not included. All MMS pipeline linear features that do not enter the Louisiana Coastal Zone were not included. For the purpose of edgematching at the State/Federal boundary, only LGS digital pipeline linear features were spatially adjusted (Figure 3.1 and Table 4.3). All edge-matching adjustments were made under MMS advisement. The LGS pipeline attributes, as derived from 124 operator source maps, were populated into the database.

To integrate the LGS/LCZ pipelines into the MMS pipeline data set, eight steps were taken to conduct this data migration and database construction.

1. Pipeline data were exported for each company from InfoCAD and imported into Intergraph Modular GIS Environment (MGE) as design files (.dgn format). Geospatial line processing and corrections were performed using Intergraph MGE.

2. The pipeline design files were exported from MGE and translated into ESRI ArcInfo coverage format. Topology for the pipeline coverage files was built using the ArcInfo "Build" command. These ArcInfo files were projected into Universal Transverse Mercator (UTM), Zone 15 coordinate system, as referenced to the North American Datum of 1983. These data were then imported into ESRI ArcView shapefile format (.shp), one shapefile for each pipeline company. In ArcView all pipeline feature records for each company shapefile were attributed with the company's name.

3. These individual company shapefiles were merged with an MMS pipeline shapefile, which had been translated from the ArcInfo export (.e00) file provided by MMS. The zone of overlapping LGS and MMS pipeline data was examined thoroughly to identify connecting pipelines. A list of MMS segment numbers was compiled for all "MMS pipeline segments" that were thought to possibly connect with "LGS pipelines." From the list of MMS pipeline segment numbers, the MMS made available to LGS photocopies of the source maps that pipeline operators had submitted to them. These photocopies were used, along with LGS operator source maps, to verify which of the possible connecting pipelines actually connect.

4. LGS met with MMS to determine the most accurate source data for each set of connecting pipelines of a representative sample from the total number in the study. For most sets of pipelines, MMS was determined to have a more detailed and up-to-date data source for operator and product. Also, the MMS pipeline data source maps submitted by the pipeline operators had been certified by licensed surveyors. Pipeline data source maps submitted by the pipeline operators to the LGS had not been certified. Therefore, the decision was made to modify the LGS digital pipeline features to connect with those of the MMS data when edge-matching sets of connecting pipelines.

5. Edge matching proceeded in ArcView using the rule established in the fourth step. Five different types of spatial modifications were employed to edge match. See Figure 3.1 for descriptions of these different types.

6. These new ArcView shapefiles needed to have a database structure that would include the MMS database definition, as provided by MMS in ArcInfo export (.e00) format. This task was achieved by merging the LGS shapefiles with the MMS shapefile (see the fourth step, above). Then, the linear pipeline features in each ArcView shapefile were attributed with information taken directly from each company's source maps. Table 3.1 shows the data fields attributed for each pipeline segment.

7. Quality control was performed by comparing the digital data with the source maps.

8. The final pipeline ArcView shapefile was translated into both ArcInfo coverage (Pipelines) and ArcInfo exchange file formats (Pipelines.e00). ArcView shapefile, ArcInfo coverage and ArcInfo export files of these pipeline and terminal or facility GIS data sets are included in the CD-ROM deliverable.

1.	-- LGS ... FIX — MMS	**Extension:** Pipelines were in alignment, but there was a gap between them. During the process of edge matching we connected a line between these end points, thus connecting the LGS and MMS pipelines.
2.	-- LGS ... FIX — MMS	**Adjustment:** The Pipelines were either overlapping or running parallel to each other along the same route. In this case, we accepted the MMS pipeline as it is. We shortened the LGS pipeline, to create a gap between the LGS and MMS end points. We then connected a line between these end points, thus connecting the LGS and MMS pipelines.
3.	-- LGS ... FIX — MMS	**Overshoot Adjustment:** The pipelines were crossing each other within a few feet. On this type, we have shortened the overshooting portion of the LGS pipeline. We then connected a line between the end points, thus connecting the LGS and MMS pipelines.
4.	-- LGS ... FIX — MMS	**Turn Adjustment:** The LGS pipelines almost adjoin the MMS pipelines within a few feet, but turn to parallel the MMS lines. On this type, we have deleted parallel portion of LGS pipelines, as in the figure, then snapped to the end point of the MMS pipeline and drew a "Fix" line to connect with the LGS pipeline.
5.	-- LGS ... FIX — MMS	**Swinging:** On one occasion the pipeline was swung from one end. First, LGS hard copy was checked for accuracy and possible digitization errors. Then, MMS hard copy maps and data were investigated for the same pipeline segment. After the assessment of accuracy of LGS pipeline, the pipeline's last sub-segment was swung to correct the problem.

Figure 3.1 Different Types of Pipeline Edgematching. **LGS** = Louisiana Geological Survey pipeline, **MMS** = Minerals Management Service pipeline, and **FIX** = connecting line segment.

Table 3.1 Data Fields of Pipelines

FIELD HEADING	DESCRIPTION
Segment_nu	Identification number of pipeline segments
Statuts_cod	Status code of pipelines
Ppl_size_c	Diameter of pipelines
Prod_code	Code of products carried by pipelines
Operator	Pipeline operator name
Quality	Quality of data source
Date	Source data creation date
Compiled_by	Source of digital compilation

3.5 Task 5 - Investigation of Pipeline Termini

All LGS/OCS connecting pipelines in the final shapefile (pipeline.shp) that originate in the OCS were traced to their "endpoints" in the LCZ by studying the operator's source maps. A pipeline endpoint represents the point beyond which further tracing of a pipeline was not necessary or beyond the scope of this project. For the former case, further tracing was not necessary because a pipeline "terminus" had been found. In the latter case, further tracing was beyond the scope of this project because a pipeline "interconnection" had been reached.

- Endpoints characterized as pipeline "termini," meet the definition given in the project Scope of Work and elaborated here: "document the routes of OCS-related pipelines to either" the northern boundary of the Louisiana Coastal Zone, the Louisiana/Mississippi state boundary, the Louisiana/Texas state boundary, "tanker terminals or refineries, whichever comes first."

- Endpoints characterized as pipeline "interconnections," represent the points past which the OCS-related pipelines could be traced no further. Whenever OCS-related pipelines leave the coastal zone, re-enter it, and exit once again, the final exit point of the LCZ was characterized as a terminus and the entire pipeline is included in the GIS including those segments outside the coastal zone.

During field investigations (GPS) coordinate positions for the pipeline endpoints, within the LCZ, were collected using a Magellan Mark Pro X DGPS receiver. Also, digital photographs of endpoint facilities were taken during field truthing. If an endpoint facility was recognized on an operator's source map, but couldn't be verified in the field due to inaccessibility, the facility was referred to as "Documented" in the "Source" field. If an endpoint facility was not recognized on an operator's source map, but identified in the field, the facility was referred to as "Undocumented" in the "Source" field. If an endpoint facility was recognized on an operator's source map, and also located in the field, the facility was referred to as "Verified" in the "Source" field.

The GPS data were downloaded into a GIS workstation and converted into ArcView GIS shapefiles; then the attribute data tables were populated. The LGS pipeline exit points on both LA/TX and LA/MS boundaries and the LCZ northern boundary were located by creating points at the intersections of the pipelines and these boundaries, then merged with the GPS data points to produce the pipeline termini ArcView shapefile (termini.shp).

Table 3.2 describes the attribute data compiled within the ArcView attribute tables associated with the two Shapefiles that represent pipeline endpoints, termini.shp and interconnections.shp. These attribute data of the pipeline termini includes termini identification codes, operator's names, locations, parishes, geographic latitudes and longitudes, mailing addresses, contact phone numbers, and fax numbers. As much of these data as possible were verified during the field investigations. Information that could not be obtained in the field was found by reference to directories of pipeline operators and confirmed by telephone contact, whenever possible.

In the telephone interviews of pipeline facility operators, some operators gave us a quick response releasing information we requested, some did not and even refused to provide additional information. The information related to pipeline termini were then "verified" and/or "documented" based on the most recently available findings. Table 4.6 provides a listing of all of the pipeline terminus facilities that were located in the Louisiana Coastal Zone.

Table 3.2 – Data Fields of Pipeline Termini

FIELD HEADING	DISCRIPTION
Tp_num	Unique number assigned to identify a terminus.
Name	Name of facility represented by a Terminus point.
Type	Type of facility represented by a Terminus point.
Parish	Name of parish in which Terminus is located.
Image	Pathname of digital image used to hotlink in ArcView.
Source	Terminus classification code.
City	Name of city where facility operator is located.
Zip	Zip code for operator address.
Telephone	Telephone number for Terminus operator's contact person.
Phone_ext	Telephone extension number of Terminus operator's contact.
Addresses	Mailing address for Terminus operator's contact person.
2_Address	Alternate address for Terminus operator's contact person.
Fax_num	Fax number for Terminus operator's contact person.
X_coord	X coordinate for the GPS point.
Y_coord	Y coordinate for the GPS point.

As mentioned above, the terminus data (termini.shp) include points where pipelines exit the LCZ by intersecting the Louisiana/Mississippi state boundary, Louisiana/Texas state boundary, the northern boundary of the LCZ, or where the pipeline terminates at a facility within the LCZ.

For all *termini* that represent facilities, the *Type* field includes *refinery* or a *tanker terminal*. The points where pipelines exit the LCZ were attributed as *Exit* in the *Source* field.

GPS field crews also collected digital photographs of the accessible pipeline facilities (see Figure 3.2 for an example). The users will be able to view these photographs by using the "hot-link" function and clicking on the points that represent facilities in the ArcView project, provided on the deliverable CD-ROM. Please note that the GPS locations and digital photographs were captured at the entrance to the facilities. Therefore, there is a geospatial offset between the end of a pipeline and the point symbol representing the facility. In two cases, the BP Elmer Station and the Chevron Venice Refinery, the distance between the two was estimated to be over 1000 meters.

Figure 3.2 Determining Geographic Position of a Pipeline Facility with GPS

The final ArcView shapefile of pipeline termini was translated into an ArcInfo coverage (Ptgeo83) and an ArcInfo exchange file (Ptgeo83.e00). Only those pipelines originating in the OCS areas and entering the LCZ, which have been reported to the LGS by pipeline operators, were traced and reported in this study. The methodology of this project is summarized in Figure 3.3.

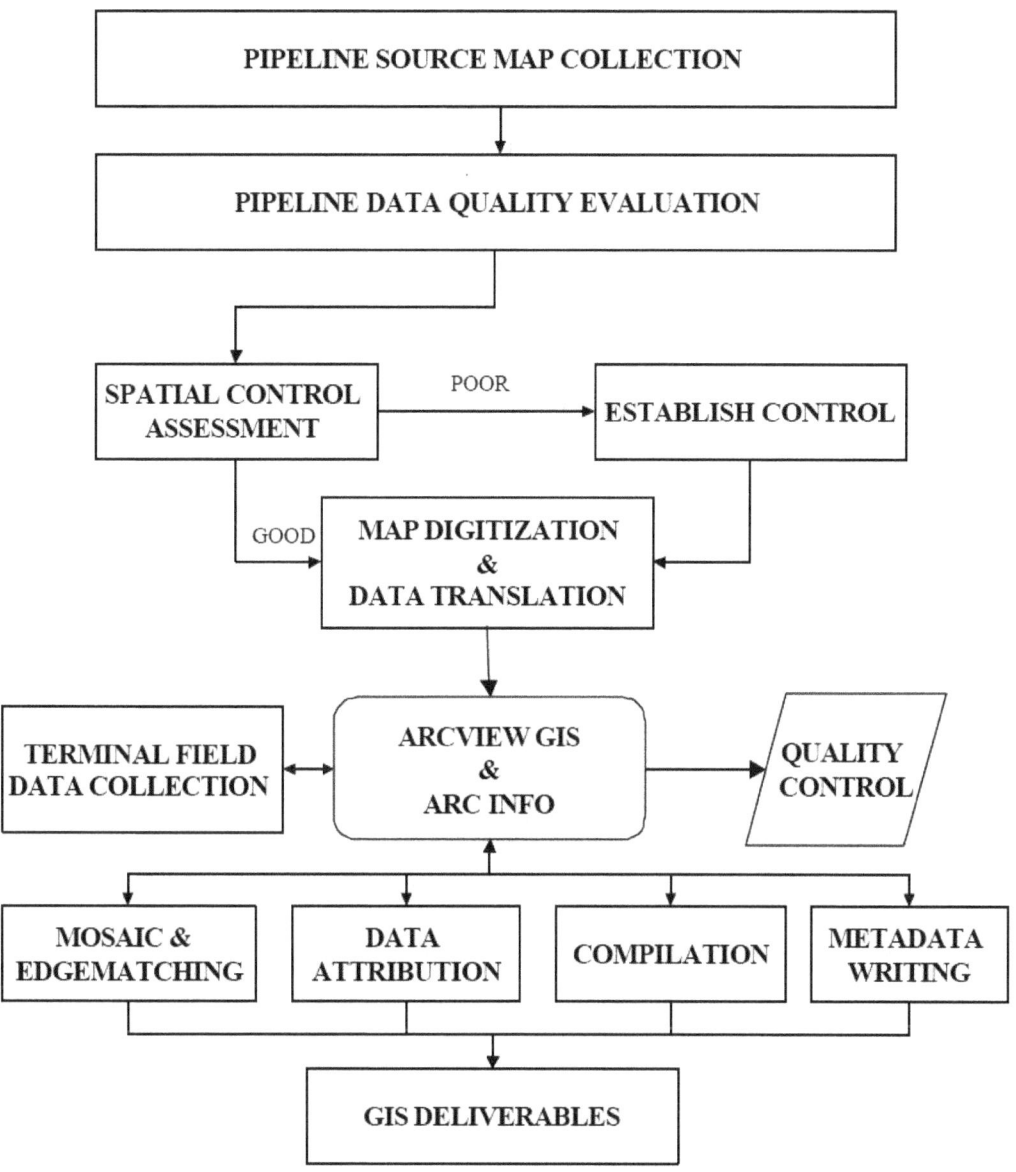

Figure 3.3 Development Methodology for Pipeline and Termini GIS Deliverables.

4.0 Results

4.1 Findings

Pipelines

Geospatial control was established for 118 source maps supplied by pipeline operators. Table 4.1 summarizes the number of maps per operator georeferenced in this project.

Table 4.1 Maps Controlled

Columbia Gulf Transmission, Inc.	88
Genesis Pipeline, USA	9
Explorer Pipeline, Co.	7
Egan Gas Storage	5
Cornerstone	4
Southern Natural Gas	2
Liquid Carbonic Specialty Gas, Corp.	1
Louisiana Natural Pipeline, Inc.	1
Delhi	1
Total Maps Controlled	**118**

A total of 214 LGS in-house source maps, from 15 companies, were digitized and compiled into the LGS digital pipeline system. Table 4.2 summarizes the number of maps digitized per company. Of the maps from pipeline operators, Columbia Gulf Transmission, Inc. and ANR Pipeline Corporation account for over 70 % of the total number of maps digitized.

Table 4.2 Maps Digitized

Columbia Gulf Transmission, Inc	88
ANR Pipeline, Co.	64
Genesis Pipeline, USA	15
Explorer Pipeline, Co.	11
Plantation Pipeline, Co.	11
ARCO Pipeline Co.	6
Egan Gas Storage	5
Cornerstone	4
Florida Gas Transmission, Co.	2
American Reserve Corp.	2
Southern Natural Gas	2
Continental	1
Delhi	1
Louisiana Natural Gas Pipeline, Inc.	1
Liquid Carbonic Specialty Gas Corp.	1
Total Maps Digitized	**214**

Table 4.3 summarizes the number of pipelines that were edge-matched per company.

Table 4.3 Pipelines Edgematched

Chevron	22
Exxon	2
Freeport	4
Koch	3
Mobil	1
Natural Gas	1
Southern Natural Gas	5
Texas Eastern Transmission	1
Shell	1
Quintana	1
Total Pipelines Edge-matched	**41**

There were 150 OCS pipelines crossing the state/federal boundary for which no onshore linking pipeline could be determined. Incomplete digital pipeline data onshore accounts for most of these, although cartographic error, abandoned pipelines, or spatial error among the OCS data may contribute.

Seven pipelines digitized onshore by LGS cross the state/federal boundary with no apparent corresponding OCS pipeline. OCS data may be incomplete or either data set may include cartographic or geospatial errors.

Pipeline Endpoints

Pipeline *endpoints* represent the points at which the pipeline tracing actually ends. These points fall into two categories, pipeline *interconnections* and pipeline *termini*. The pipeline interconnections are simply points beyond which further tracing of those pipelines, by using the source maps, was prevented by the interconnection of multiple pipelines. Though these interconnection pipeline endpoints are not pipeline termini, they have been included on the deliverable CD-ROM in ArcView Shapefile format (interconnections.shp).

The pipeline termini are defined as points where the pipelines exit the Louisiana Coastal Zone by crossing either the northern boundary of the LCZ, the Louisiana/Mississippi state boundary, the Louisiana/Texas state boundary, or *tanker terminals* or *refineries* within the LCZ. These pipeline termini are defined by the MMS and have been included on the accompanying CD-ROM, in ArcView Shapefile format (termini.shp).

Table 4.4 shows a total of 42 pipeline termini, located by GPS field surveying

Table 4.4 Located Termini

Refinery	4
Tanker Terminal	15
Northern boundary exits	21
State border exits	2
Located Termini	**42**

Table 4.5 shows a list of companies operating the pipeline termini facilities, identified and located in the field, using GPS. All MMS/OCS-associated pipelines crossing the LCZ were attributed with data retrieved from the operator's source maps. A total of 19 OCS-related pipeline termini were identified and located by GPS field positioning. Of these, 18 were recognized on operator's source maps and located in the field using GPS, and referred to as "Verified" in the *Source* field of the database. One of them is *Undocumented*, meaning the facility was not recognized on an operator's source map, but was identified in the field. These terminus facilities were identified, located, and photographed in the field by the GPS crew so that descriptive information could be reported.

Table 4.5 Terminus Facility Operators

ANR Pipe Line Co.	1
BP Exploration Inc.	1
Chevron Pipeline Co.	3
Exxon Pipeline Co.	3
Freeport McMoran Oil & Gas Co.	1
Louisiana Interstate Gas Co.	1
Marathon Pipeline Co.	2
Mobil Pipeline Co.	1
Shell Petroleum Co.	1
Sea Robin (Southern Natural Gas Co.)	2
El Paso/Tennessee Gas Pipeline Co.	1
Transcontinental Gas Pipeline Co.	1
Western Gas Resources Co.	1
Total Terminal	**19**

Table 4.6 provides a listing of all of the pipeline terminus facilities that were located in the Louisiana Coastal Zone.

Table 4.6 Pipeline Terminus Facilities

Facility	Type	Parish	Phone
BP Elmer Station	Tanker Terminal	Jefferson	713-599-8114
Chevron Fourchon	Tanker Terminal	Lafourche	
Chevron Ostrica	Tanker Terminal	Plaquemines	504-364-2189
Chevron Venice	Refinery	Plaquemines	504-364-2189
El Paso/Tennessee Gas Pipeline	Tanker Terminal	Terrebonne	713-757-2500
Exxon Delta	Tanker Terminal	Plaquemines	713-656-2709
Exxon Grand Isle Station	Tanker Terminal	Jefferson	713-656-9579
Exxon South Bend	Tanker Terminal	St. Mary	713-656-2709
Freeport McMoran	Tanker Terminal	Jefferson	504-582-1853
Johnson Bayou Facility	Tanker Terminal	Cameron	
Louisiana Interstate Gas	Tanker Terminal	Terrebonne	
Lowry Dock	Tanker Terminal	Cameron	318-232-3053
Marathon Venice	Tanker Terminal	Plaquemines	713-629-6600
Marathon West Delta	Tanker Terminal	Plaquemines	713-629-6600
Sea Robin	Tanker Terminal	Vermillion	205-325-749
Sea Robin	Tanker Terminal	Vermillion	205-325-749
Shell Western	Refinery	St. Bernard	
Transco Cameron Meadow	Refinery	Cameron	
Western Gas Resources	Refinery	St. Bernard	303-252-3363

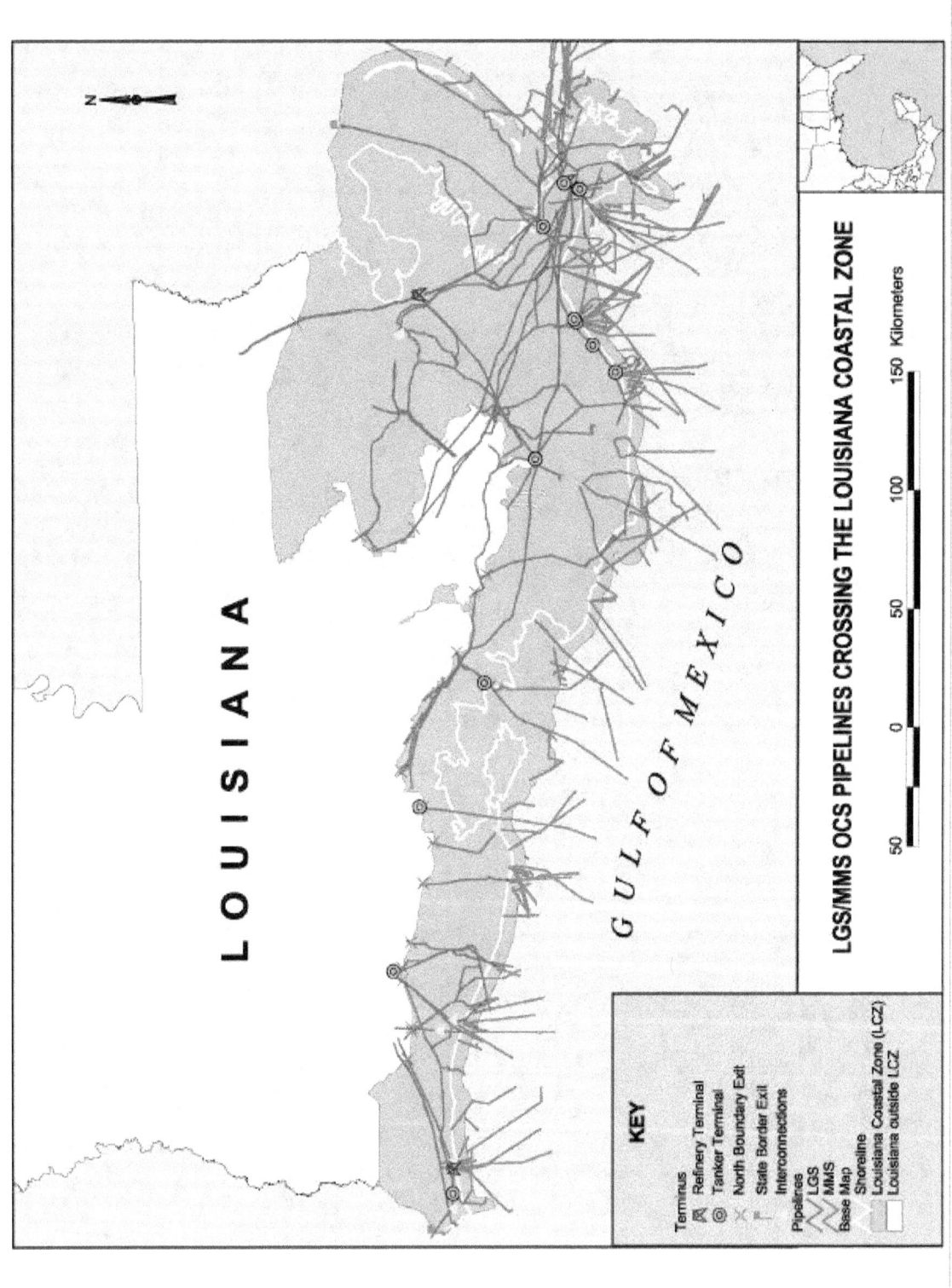

Figure 4.1 OCS Pipelines Crossing the Louisiana Coastal Zone.

4.2 Problems and Solutions

A major problem was to edge-match spatial positions of the MMS/OCS digital pipelines and the LGS digital pipelines along the state/federal water boundary. The pipeline operator's source maps were submitted to the LGS voluntarily and with certification. The data quality of some source maps was believed to be less accurate than that of others. The authors met with the MMS Pipeline Group to determine how to resolve edgematching problems. MMS and LGS agreed on the following resolution methods:

1. LGS pipelines were spatially adjusted for edgematching with the MMS pipelines whenever the pipelines were confirmed to match with each other. Since the data submitted to MMS by the pipeline companies was certified as being correct, and the data submitted to LGS was not, the MMS pipelines remain spatially unchanged. See Section 3.4 for a detailed discussion of this process.

2. The spatial adjustment of the LGS pipelines, company by company, was carried out, and they were populated with attribute data in the same way as other LGS pipelines.

3. They were then merged with the MMS pipeline data using ArcView GIS and translated into ArcInfo GIS format.

Another problem was encountered during the field investigations of the facilities at the pipeline endpoints. The GPS locations were captured at the main entrances to the facilities. These are not the usual entrances for pipelines; therefore, there is a geospatial offset between the end of a pipeline and the point symbol representing the facility. In two cases, the "BP Elmer Station" and the "Chevron Venice Refinery," the entrance to the facility property is estimated to be over 1000 meters form the physical pipeline terminus. The GPS positional coordinates located during the field survey have not been adjusted.

5.0 Conclusions

In this study, the Louisiana Geological Survey (LGS) and the Minerals Management Service (MMS) of the U.S. Department of the Interior have pooled resources to produce compatible, public domain, pipeline data for a number of the pipelines in the Louisiana Coastal Zone. These data should prove mutually beneficial to both state and federal governments. LGS has established an effective methodology for developing OCS-related pipeline GIS data for the Louisiana Coastal Zone (LCZ) by combining GIS data from these two public organizations and contributing an additional research effort. Due to an incomplete collection of operator source maps, the OCS pipeline GIS data produced, as a deliverable for this project, is not a complete inventory of the OCS-related pipelines that pass through the LCZ. With the current methodology established, future additions to these data should prove to be more efficient.

All of the pipelines represented with the LGS Pipeline GIS, that are within the LCZ and cross the Louisiana's state-federal boundary, have been combined with all 191 of the pipelines represented in the MMS Pipeline GIS that cross the Louisiana's state-federal boundary into the LCZ. These combined pipeline data have been edgematched to produce the resulting 198 OCS-related pipelines in the LCZ. Wherever possible, these pipelines have been traced to their *termini* within the LCZ. The pipeline and pipeline termini data described above, constitute the deliverable GIS data for this study. Federal Geographic Data Committee (FGDC) compliant metadata files can be found on the accompanying CD-ROM, along with the deliverable GIS data.

There are 150 pipelines, of the 191 total in the MMS data crossing the boundary into the LCZ, which could not be matched with pipelines in the LGS data. There are 7 pipelines in the LGS data crossing the state-federal boundary into federal waters, which could not be matched with pipelines in the MMS data.

Assuming that that the MMS GIS of pipelines in the federal waters near Louisiana are complete, the deliverable MMS/OCS pipeline GIS for the LCZ contains edgmatched LGS/OCS pipelines for approximately 21.5% of the total 191. However, the fact that there are 7 LGS pipelines with no matches in the MMS data indicates that there might be other pipelines missing from the MMS data. If this is the case, this estimate of completeness should be lower. When these 7 LGS pipelines are included the estimate of completion is 20.7%. Considering that the LGS pipeline GIS data are not yet complete for the LCZ, the percentage of completion could be further reduced, slightly.

Pipeline operators will continue to submit pipeline data to the LGS, in its capacity as the Louisiana Repository of the National Pipeline Mapping System. The remaining pipeline data, yet to be submitted, could provide the missing data needed to complete this MMS/OCS pipeline GIS for the LCZ, over the next couple of years.

6.0 Recommendations

Throughout the extensive studies of modern environmental impacts in Louisiana's Coastal Zone, pipelines have often been implicated as a significant contributor. Unfortunately, no comprehensive, accurate record of pipeline routes exists for the LCZ. Documenting the complex network of pipeline systems that have been developed is an essential step towards researching and understanding the roles that pipelines have played in the deterioration of Louisiana's Coastal Zone.

The accompanying pipeline GIS database for the LCZ is a substantial initial step toward developing a comprehensive oil and gas pipeline GIS for the Louisiana Coastal Zone. This collaboration of effort will prove to be a substantial benefit, not only to the collaborating organizations, but also to the entire pipeline community. However, further work is needed to complete the compilation of a comprehensive pipeline GIS for the LCZ. Unfortunately, approximately 50% of the pipeline operator's source maps have not yet been provided to state or federal governments. The LGS is currently collaborating with the U.S. Department of Transportation, Office of Pipeline Safety in the development of the National Pipeline Mapping System through the year 2003. This project is providing major additions to the LGS pipeline GIS for Louisiana.

Future completion and maintenance of the pipeline GIS for the LCZ will require a collaborative effort of federal, state and local governmental agencies, public universities, and the pipeline industry. Only in an atmosphere of cooperation among these groups can the completion of an accurate pipeline GIS for the Louisiana Coastal Zone be coordinated within the next few years and maintained through future years.

The authors recommend the following.

1) Louisiana pipeline regulators at DNR should facilitate the acquisition of pipeline operator source maps from those operators, in Louisiana, who have not yet submitted information to state or federal agencies, this would be a major contribution.

2) The MMS fund a follow up field investigation, to research and document the remaining, OCS-related pipelines and terminus facilities that have been revealed as being undocumented, by this study.

3) A viable program for continued maintenance of these pipeline GIS data should be designed and implemented within the existing framework of the governments of the State of Louisiana and the United States of America, with cooperation from companies that operate or construct pipelines in the Louisiana Coastal Zone.

7.0 Deliverables

7.1 Final Report

This document summarizes the procedures used and the results, conclusions, and recommendations that were detailed during the preparation of GIS deliverables for the project, "Research, Compilation, and Digitization of Problematical and Uncontrolled Source Maps for the Louisiana Statewide Oil and Gas Pipeline Digital Database."

> Peele R.H., J.I. Snead, and W. Feng, 2002. Outer Continental Shelf Pipelines Crossing the Louisiana Coastal Zone: A Geographic Information System Approach. A final report for the U.S. Department of the Interior, Minerals Management Service, Gulf of Mexico OCS Region, Metairie, LA. Cooperative Agreement No. 1185-01-97-CA-30895.

A digital copy of the report is on the CD-ROM.

7.2 Technical Summary

A Technical Summary has been prepared for delivery with the final report as per MMS guidelines.

7.3 GIS Data

The principal products desired by the COTR are the ArcInfo GIS files produced by this project. Those data have been delivered to MMS on a CD-ROM and may be available, via the Internet, at the conclusion of the project.

> Peele R. H., W. Feng, and J.I. Snead, 2002. Outer Continental Shelf Pipelines Crossing the Louisiana Coastal Zone: A Geographic Information System CD-ROM. A CD-ROM containing the GIS data in both ArcView and ArcInfo formats for the U.S. Department of the Interior, Minerals Management Service Gulf of Mexico OCS Region, Metairie, LA Cooperative Agreement No. 1185-01-98-CA-30895.

7.4 Hard Copy Plots

Large inkjet plots of the GIS pipeline data have been included as deliverables.

7.5 Slide Presentation

A Microsoft PowerPoint slide presentation summary of the project has also been prepared as per MMS request. Both a digital copy, on the CD-ROM, and a hard copy have been included.

The Department of the Interior Mission

As the Nation's principal conservation agency, the Department of the Interior has responsibility for most of our nationally owned public lands and natural resources. This includes fostering sound use of our land and water resources; protecting our fish, wildlife, and biological diversity; preserving the environmental and cultural values of our national parks and historical places; and providing for the enjoyment of life through outdoor recreation. The Department assesses our energy and mineral resources and works to ensure that their development is in the best interests of all our people by encouraging stewardship and citizen participation in their care. The Department also has a major responsibility for American Indian reservation communities and for people who live in island territories under U.S. administration.

The Minerals Management Service Mission

As a bureau of the Department of the Interior, the Minerals Management Service's (MMS) primary responsibilities are to manage the mineral resources located on the Nation's Outer Continental Shelf (OCS), collect revenue from the Federal OCS and onshore Federal and Indian lands, and distribute those revenues.

Moreover, in working to meet its responsibilities, the **Offshore Minerals Management Program** administers the OCS competitive leasing program and oversees the safe and environmentally sound exploration and production of our Nation's offshore natural gas, oil and other mineral resources. The MMS **Minerals Revenue Management** meets its responsibilities by ensuring the efficient, timely and accurate collection and disbursement of revenue from mineral leasing and production due to Indian tribes and allottees, States and the U.S. Treasury.

The MMS strives to fulfill its responsibilities through the general guiding principles of: (1) being responsive to the public's concerns and interests by maintaining a dialogue with all potentially affected parties and (2) carrying out its programs with an emphasis on working to enhance the quality of life for all Americans by lending MMS assistance and expertise to economic development and environmental protection.